Rabbits and Rainbows

written by Margaret Hillert

illustrated by Judy Hand

For Lynn, who listens

Library of Congress Catalog Card No. 84-052173
Copyright © 1985 by Margaret Hillert.
Published by The STANDARD PUBLISHING Company, Cincinnati, Ohio.
Division of STANDEX INTERNATIONAL Corporation. Printed in U.S.A.

A LITTLE PRAYER

A little prayer at morning
Will start the day just right.
Another one at bedtime
Will see you through the night.
And anytime between time,
Whatever you may do,
You'll find it goes much better
With a little prayer from you.

I'M SINGING

A little bird is singing
Away up in the tree,
And I am feeling happy,
As happy as can be.
I'm singing, too, and dancing,
So light of heart and free.
Because God made the little bird
And spring and song and me.

GROWING THINGS

If you want to grow a seed,
Here's a list of things you need.
A hole of course is number one.
Then comes rain and air and sun.
Maybe fertilizer, too,
And a little prayer from you.
For to grow up through the sod,
Seeds need all these things from God.

DUCK IN THE RAIN

Soft red rubbers
    and raincoat of yellow,
What a fine outfit
    for this little fellow.
He's shining and wet
    from his tail to his crown,
And he's quacking his thanks
    for the rain pouring down.

RAINBOW PROMISE

A rainbow is a promise
That God made long ago.
I like to see it in the sky
And watch its colors glow.

I couldn't make a rainbow
For everyone to see,
But I can keep my promises
To friends and family.

TRY IT

The little things
I try myself,
I soon can do
All by myself.
But if I should
Have any doubt,
A little prayer
Will help me out.

NEW BABY

My baby brother is brand new.
His eyes are sort of darkish blue.
He's all curled up and pretty small.
He hasn't any hair at all.
But when he grabs my finger tight
And squeezes it with all his might,
I'm sure he likes me, and I know
We'll have fun when he starts to grow.
I'll let him share in all I do.
I'll read him Bible stories, too.

EYES

Thank You, Lord, for eyes to see
Starlings in the maple tree,
Sun by day, and moon by night,
Snowflakes tiny, rainbows bright,
Flowers, grass, and skies of blue,
Puppy dogs and kittens, too,
And, in a puddle, even me!
Thank You, Lord, for eyes to see.

HANDS

Thank You, Lord, for hands to hold
Apples red and pumpkins gold,
Shells and starfish, little rocks,
Hammer, nails, and building blocks.
Hands to catch and throw a ball
And help when baby starts to fall.
Hands that fold themselves to pray.
Thank You for my hands today.

LEGS

Thank You, Lord, for legs to run
Through puddles shining in the sun.
Legs to climb a hill and then
Scramble down the hill again.
Legs to race and rush and roam.
Legs to hurry me back home.
Legs to kneel when day is done.
Thank You, Lord, for legs to run.

VISITING

I like it when we visit God
In Sunday morning prayer.
I like the people in His house
With friends and family there.
I like the songs and stories, too.
I listen quietly.
And when I get back home again,
Why, then, God visits me.

WILD RABBIT

It isn't often that you meet
A bunny rabbit on the street
But yesterday we did.
He stopped ahead a square or two
So we could get a close-up view
Before he hopped and hid.
We saw the sun shine through his ear
And then he sensed that we were near
And skittered out of sight.
Although he was a lovely brown
With fur as soft as thistledown,
His little tail was white.
On earth below, in skies above
God made small things for us to love.

WHAT I AM

When I wrinkle my nose, I'm a rabbit.
When I gallop around, I'm a horse.
When I dive and I splash
And I flip and I flash,
I'm being a fish, of course.

When I snuffle and snort, I'm a dragon.
When I roar, I'm a lion that's wild.
But at nighttime instead,
By the side of my bed,
When I'm saying my prayers, I'm a child.

MY TEDDY BEAR

A teddy bear is nice to hold.
The one I have is getting old.
His paws are almost wearing out
And so's his funny furry snout
From rubbing on my nose of skin.
And all his fur is pretty thin.
A ribbon and a piece of string
Make a sort of necktie thing.
His eyes came out and now instead
He has some new ones made of thread.
I take him everywhere I go
And tell him all the things I know.
I like the way he feels at night
All snuggled up against me tight,
And so in every bedtime prayer
I'm thankful for my teddy bear.